Snowshoe Cats as Pets

A Complete Snowshoe Cat Owner Guide

Snowshoe Cat Information, Where to Buy, Care, Behavior, Cost, Health, Training, Grooming, Diet and a whole lot more!

By Lolly Brown

Copyrights and Trademarks

All rights reserved. No part of this book may be reproduced or transformed in any form or by any means, graphic, electronic, or mechanical, including photocopying, recording, taping, or by any information storage retrieval system, without the written permission of the author.

This publication is Copyright ©2016. Nevada. All products, graphics, publications, software and services mentioned and recommended in this publication are protected by trademarks. In such instance, all trademarks & copyright belong to the respective owners. For information consult www.NRBpublishing.com

Disclaimer and Legal Notice

This product is not legal, medical, or accounting advice and should not be interpreted in that manner. You need to do your own due-diligence to determine if the content of this product is right for you. While every attempt has been made to verify the information shared in this publication, neither the author, neither publisher, nor the affiliates assume any responsibility for errors, omissions or contrary interpretation of the subject matter herein. Any perceived slights to any specific person(s) or organization(s) are purely unintentional.

We have no control over the nature, content and availability of the web sites listed in this book. The inclusion of any web site links does not necessarily imply a recommendation or endorse the views expressed within them. We take no responsibility for, and will not be liable for, the websites being temporarily unavailable or being removed from the internet.

The accuracy and completeness of information provided herein and opinions stated herein are not guaranteed or warranted to produce any particular results, and the advice and strategies, contained herein may not be suitable for every individual. Neither the author nor the publisher shall be liable for any loss incurred as a consequence of the use and application, directly or indirectly, of any information presented in this work. This publication is designed to provide information in regard to the subject matter covered.

Neither the author nor the publisher assume any responsibility for any errors or omissions, nor do they represent or warrant that the ideas, information, actions, plans, suggestions contained in this book is in all cases accurate. It is the reader's responsibility to find advice before putting anything written in this book into practice. The information in this book is not intended to serve as legal, medical, or accounting advice.

Foreword

Snowshoe cats were admired by pet owners mainly for their unique "grumpy" appearance yet sweet and affectionate attitude. Some people say that they are the best of both worlds! They may look angry and judgmental on the outside but they are truly mellow and loving on the inside. Interesting right?

Although Snowshoes are truly a great choice as pets, these cats doesn't come with a thin instruction manual, but fear not! In this book you'll be easily guided on understanding your Snowshoe pet, their behaviors, their characteristics, how you should feed and care for them and a whole lot more.

Embark on a wonderful journey of sharing your life with a Snowshoe cat. Learn to maximize the great privilege of living with one and be able to share this unique and unforgettable experience just like many interesting cat owners that came before you!

Table of Contents

Introduction 9
    Glossary of Cat Terms 11
Chapter One: Understanding Snowshoe Cats 17
    Facts about Snowshoe Cats 18
    Quick Facts 20
    History of Snowshoe Cats 21
Chapter Two: Before You Buy a Snowshoe 25
    License Requirements 26
    Snowshoe Cats Behavior with Children and Pets 29
    How Many Snowshoe Cats Should You Keep? 30
    How Much Does it Cost to Keep a Snowshoe Cat? 31
    Initial Costs 32
    Monthly Costs 36
    Pros and Cons of Snowshoe Cats 39
Chapter Three: Tips in Buying Snowshoe Cats 41
    Finding a Reputable Snowshoe Breeder 42
    Selecting a Healthy Snowshoe 49
Chapter Four: Maintenance for Snowshoe Cats 51
    Tips on How to Cat-Proof Your Home 52
    Environmental Requirements for Snowshoe Cats 53
    Toys and Accessories for Snowshoe Cats 54

Tips in Keeping Your Cats Happy Indoors and 56

Chapter Five: Nutritional Needs of Snowshoe Cats 57

....57

Essential Nutrients 58

Toxic Foods to Avoid 61

Types of Commercial Cat Foods 63

Food Additives 64

Tips in Selecting a High-Quality Cat Food Brand 64

How to Feed Your Snowshoe Cats 67

Chapter Six: Caring Guidelines for Snowshoe Cats..............73

Socializing Your Cat..74

Training Your Snowshoe Cats 75

Behavioral Problems 79

Grooming Snowshoe Cats..81

Presenting Your Snowshoe Cat...83

Preparing Your Snowshoe Cat for Show 86

Chapter Seven: Breeding Snowshoe Cats 89

Basic Cat Breeding Information 90

Mating Behavior of Cats 91

Mating Time Period 92

Chapter Eight: Keeping Your Cat Healthy 95

Common Health Problems...96

Recommended Vaccinations for Snowshoes 104

Signs of Possible Illnesses 108

Chapter Nine: Snowshoe Cats Checklist 111

Basic Cat Information 112

Nutritional Needs 113

Breeding Information 114

Cat Accessories 115

Index 117

PHOTOS 123

REFERENCES 125

Introduction

Snowshoe cats are quite unique not only because of their personality and distinct characteristics but also because of their origin. Snowshoes are sort of procreated and discovered by "accident." Interesting isn't it? These species are made out of two different cat breeds fueled by a pet owner's curiosity and made popular by passion during the 1960's.

Although Snowshoe cats have only existed for about 45 years, they are a rare breed with a distinct characteristic that will surely bring out the best in you and will truly serve you a purpose. They also have a reputation of being sociable

Introduction

and they don't like being left alone, despite of that grumpy face.

These cats are medium in size, and usually have a smooth coat with white feet, hence its name. They are the offspring of a Siamese and American Shorthair cats. Some cat enthusiasts and owners try to breed a Siamese with other bi-color cat species, resulting in a Snowshoe cats that only vary in its point coloration or coat markings.

Snowshoes are great as pets, though sometimes some people may find their attitudes very intimidating, but that's of course, part of who they are. They are smart and can be easily trained like other cat. Although, Snowshoes are generally easy to care for, you will still need some useful tips and guidance, especially if you want to try breeding them because these cats are very rare and quite hard to find.

Snowshoe cats definitely last for a longtime! These cats have a lifespan of 20 years and more! Now that's for keeps! They're great longtime companions, and because of that you need some guidance on how to take care of them, train them and possibly bring out the best in them so that they can also bring out the better part of you!

Fortunately, this ultimate guide will teach you on how to be the best Snowshoe owner you can be! Inside this book, you will find tons of helpful information about Snowshoe cats; how they live, how to deal with them and realize the great benefits of owning one!

Introduction

Glossary of Cat Terms

Abundism – Referring to a cat that has markings more prolific than is normal.

Acariasis – A type of mite infection.

ACF – Australian Cat Federation

Affix – A cattery name that follows the cat's registered name; cattery owner, not the breeder of the cat.

Agouti – A type of natural coloring pattern in which individual hairs have bands of light and dark coloring.

Ailurophile – A person who loves cats.

Albino – A type of genetic mutation which results in little to no pigmentation, in the eyes, skin, and coat.

Allbreed – Referring to a show that accepts all breeds or a judge who is qualified to judge all breeds.

Alley Cat – A non-pedigreed cat.

Alter – A desexed cat; a male cat that has been neutered or a female that has been spayed.

Amino Acid – The building blocks of protein; there are 22 types for cats, 11 of which can be synthesized and 11 which must come from the diet (see essential amino acid).

Anestrus – The period between estrus cycles in a female cat.

Introduction

Any Other Variety (AOV) – A registered cat that doesn't conform to the breed standard.

ASH – American Shorthair, a breed of cat.

Back Cross – A type of breeding in which the offspring is mated back to the parent.

Balance – Referring to the cat's structure; proportional in accordance with the breed standard.

Barring – Describing the tabby's striped markings.

Base Color – The color of the coat.

Bicolor – A cat with patched color and white.

Blaze – A white coloring on the face, usually in the shape of an inverted V.

Bloodline – The pedigree of the cat.

Brindle – A type of coloring, a brownish or tawny coat with streaks of another color.

Castration – The surgical removal of a male cat's testicles.

Cat Show – An event where cats are shown and judged.

Cattery – A registered cat breeder; also, a place where cats may be boarded.

CFA – The Cat Fanciers Association.

Cobby – A compact body type.

Introduction

Colony – A group of cats living wild outside.

Color Point – A type of coat pattern that is controlled by color point alleles; pigmentation on the tail, legs, face, and ears with an ivory or white coat.

Colostrum – The first milk produced by a lactating female; contains vital nutrients and antibodies.

Conformation – The degree to which a pedigreed cat adheres to the breed standard.

Cross Breed – The offspring produced by mating two distinct breeds.

Dam – The female parent.

Declawing – The surgical removal of the cat's claw and first toe joint.

Developed Breed – A breed that was developed through selective breeding and crossing with established breeds.

Down Hairs – The short, fine hairs closest to the body which keep the cat warm.

DSH – Domestic Shorthair.

Estrus – The reproductive cycle in female cats during which she becomes fertile and receptive to mating.

Fading Kitten Syndrome – Kittens that die within the first two weeks after birth; the cause is generally unknown.

Introduction

Feral – A wild, untamed cat of domestic descent.

Gestation – Pregnancy; the period during which the fetuses develop in the female's uterus.

Guard Hairs – Coarse, outer hairs on the coat.

Harlequin – A type of coloring in which there are van markings of any color with the addition of small patches of the same color on the legs and body.

Inbreeding – The breeding of related cats within a closed group or breed.

Kibble – Another name for dry cat food.

Lilac – A type of coat color that is pale pinkish-gray.

Line – The pedigree of ancestors; family tree.

Litter – The name given to a group of kittens born at the same time from a single female.

Mask – A type of coloring seen on the face in some breeds.

Matts – Knots or tangles in the cat's fur.

Mittens – White markings on the feet of a cat.

Moggie – Another name for a mixed breed cat.

Mutation – A change in the DNA of a cell.

Muzzle – The nose and jaws of an animal.

Introduction

Natural Breed – A breed that developed without selective breeding or the assistance of humans.

Neutering – Desexing a male cat.

Open Show – A show in which spectators are allowed to view the judging.

Pads – The thick skin on the bottom of the feet.

Particolor – A type of coloration in which there are markings of two or more distinct colors.

Patched – A type of coloration in which there is any solid color, tabby, or tortoiseshell color plus white.

Pedigree – A purebred cat; the cat's papers showing its family history.

Pet Quality – A cat that is not deemed of high enough standard to be shown or bred.

Piebald – A cat with white patches of fur.

Points – Also color points; markings of contrasting color on the face, ears, legs, and tail.

Pricked – Referring to ears that sit upright.

Purebred – A pedigreed cat.

Queen – An intact female cat.

Roman Nose – A type of nose shape with a bump or arch.

Introduction

Scruff – The loose skin on the back of a cat's neck.

Selective Breeding – A method of modifying or improving a breed by choosing cats with desirable traits.

Senior – A cat that is more than 5 but less than 7 years old.

Sire – The male parent of a cat.

Solid – Also self; a cat with a single coat color.

Spay – Desexing a female cat.

Stud – An intact male cat.

Tabby – A type of coat pattern consisting of a contrasting color over a ground color.

Tom Cat – An intact male cat.

Tortoiseshell – A type of coat pattern consisting of a mosaic of red or cream and another base color.

Tri-Color – A type of coat pattern consisting of three distinct colors in the coat.

Tuxedo – A black and white cat.

Unaltered – A cat that has not been desexed.

Chapter One: Understanding Snowshoe Cats

Snowshoe cats may often time look like the authoritative master or maiden of the home, your nagging mom, the late-night comedian, or the attention-seeking girlfriend. In whatever attitude or mood it appeals, you can expect it to be intelligent, energetic, and caring, although sometimes it may have a different attitude with strangers.

The Snowshoe is a unique and wonderful bred of cat but it may not be the right choice for everyone. Before you decide whether or not it might be the right pet for you and your family, you need to learn and invest a significant

Chapter One: Understanding Snowshoe Cats

amount of time in getting to know these animals. In this chapter you will receive an introduction to the Snowshoe cat breed including some basic facts and information as well as the history of the breed.

This information, in combination with the practical information about keeping Snowshoe cats in the next chapter, will help you decide if this is the cat companion for you.

Facts about Snowshoe Cats

As mentioned earlier, its unique name came from its characteristic for having white feet. The official Snowshoe coat color is light color ranging from white to flesh-colored with darker face, ears, legs, and tail otherwise known as **point** coloration, which is also the recognized color in cat associations as well as cat registries.

The ears have a slightly rounded tip which is usually medium in size and the head is typically wedge in shape or an "apple-like" shape with a traditional cat look. The ears, tail, face and legs (points) are dark or solid black-based colors with a solid white pattern in its short-haired coat. The face, chest, stomach, and paws areas are also white in color. The body is an even coloration, as well as the shoulders and hips; the chest areas have a slightly lighter shade as well as its stomach.

Chapter One: Understanding Snowshoe Cats

Paw pads vary from white, point color, flesh tone, or mottled.

As snowshoe cats age, their color will eventually get darker, reaching sort of a chocolate brown or darkish brown shade. Snowshoe cats come in a variety of colors such as blue, lilac, lynx, fawn, chocolate, and seal points with blue eyes. Its weight is generally 10 - 12 pounds, with many males reaching 14 pounds or more. It is also longer in length and wiser compared to other cats.

Breeding snowshoe cats are harder than usual; its pattern relies on recessive genes and other factors to produce desired results. That is why some of these snowshoes usually have either too much white markings or too little white, some even have scattered white on their bodies. The cats' body type is even harder to breed, to achieve a perfect breed of Snowshoe cats, means to produce the correct color and points, while still maintaining the American Shorthair's body structure and the length of the Siamese.

Snowshoes, like any other cats, are generally carnivorous. You can feed them with meat every now and then. Usually pet cats such as snowshoes can get its complete nutrients with variety of cat foods available in local pet stores and markets. The general guideline when feeding cats is that the cat food should have high and balanced levels of amino acids, vitamins, fiber, minerals and fats to maintain its health and keep it away from diseases.

Chapter One: Understanding Snowshoe Cats

In terms of its health, Snowshoes are generally healthy, although sometimes they may tend to have crossed eyes, which can be traced to its Siamese lineage. These cats could also occasionally have a tail spasm but other than that, they are not prone to illnesses, and fortunately **those common flaws don't affect its health in a major way or its ability to be a great companion provided that you as the owner can keep them** healthy and happy.

Quick Facts

- **Pedigree**: very talkative, short coat, average shedding, pointed colors
- **Breed Size**: medium to medium-large (normal size)
- **Height:** 9 - 11 inches
- **Weight**: average 10 to 14 pounds
- **Physique:** medium-sized, muscled
- **Coat Length**: short
- **Skin Texture**: soft and smooth
- **Color**: blue, lilac, lynx, fawn, chocolate, and seal points
- **Eyes**: blue colored eyes
- **Ears**: very large (2 to 3 inches tall), wide at the base
- **Tail**: medium in length; rounded tip
- **Temperament**: very energetic and interactive, sweet, affectionate and loyal

Chapter One: Understanding Snowshoe Cats

- **Strangers**: needs warming up and proper introduction
- **Children**: can bond with children
- **Behavior with other pets:** gets along with other cats and most other pets
- **Exercise Needs**: Playing with toys
- **Health Conditions**: generally healthy but prone to some conditions such as panleukopenia, calicivirus, rhinotracheitis, and rabies, feline leukemia virus (FeLV).
- **Comparable Breeds:** California Spangled Cat, Norwegian Forest Cat, Egyptian Mau
- **Lifespan**: average 15 to 20 years

History of Snowshoe Cats

As mentioned earlier Snowshoe cats' came from the Siamese family. The Siamese's distinctive characteristics appear physically on the Snowshoe's body which is light-colored combined with darker areas in its tail, legs, and ears. Another distinct physical characteristic that they got from their Siamese ancestors is its white inverted V-shaped marking between its blue eyes and over the muzzle. What makes them unique of course, is its white paws both in its mittens (front paws) and boots (rear paws).

Its coat is short hair and its body shape is more

Chapter One: Understanding Snowshoe Cats

rounded than that of the Siamese.

Snowshoes dates back to the late Victorian era around 1900's, scientists and animal experts have photographic and silk-screen evidences of Siamese kittens with four white feet. However, it's not the type of breed that we know today, modern Snowshoes species were developed in the mid-20th century. During the 1950's these cats were known as Silver Laces and back then they were still consider a Siamese breed.

In the 1960s, an ordinary cat breeder named Dorothy Hinds-Daugherty from Philadelphia "accidentally" bred a Siamese-type cat with an American Short-hair which resulted in a moderate body shape like a Siamese, and white feet, that's why she named these cats Snowshoes.

After that, she decided to try breeding some more of these Snowshoes, and started again with a a couple of white-pawed Siamese kittens, this time she mated it specifically with a domestic American Shorthair cat with tuxedo markings that has a black coat, white belly, chest, and paws as well as darker shade around its eyes. Voila! Snowshoe cats became a whole new breed. It's intelligence from both lineage and a combination of unique traits made Daugherty decides to promote it in pet shows but with no success.

Eventually, Daugherty gave up breeding Snowshoes but fortunately it intrigued the curious mind of other cat breeders and cat associations, particularly, Vikki Olander.

Chapter One: Understanding Snowshoe Cats

Olander got the support of the Cat Fanciers Federation (CFF) and the American Cat Association's (ACA) through the first ever paper he wrote about the breeding standard for Snowshoes.

In 1974, he successfully obtained an "experimental breed" status for the Snowshoe. However, by 1977, Olander struggles to keep the Snowshoe breed alive; he was the last breeder of the Snowshoe in the United States. Fortunately Jim Hoffman and Georgia Kuhnell, who were another interested breeders contacted Olander. They eventually obtained the champion status from the Cat Fanciers Federation in 1983.

By 1989, Olander left the program because her fiancé was allergic to cats. However, by then the Snowshoe had already built a strong following. The breed attained champion status with the American Cat Fanciers Association in 1990. In 1993 it was officially recognized by The International Cat Association.

In the United Kingdom, a breeding program was started in 1986. In 1998, Mollie Southall of Cattery and Maureen Shackell were two of the last breeders left. They struggle to keep the breed alive with only about five cats.

In 2006, Kelly Cruse of Destrier Cats got involved and introduces new colors and patterns. Mollie's German senior assistant, Ferry Vom Friedewald also gave the Snowshoes a completely new bloodline.

Chapter One: Understanding Snowshoe Cats

Around 2010, Snowshoe Cat Club head, Destrier Dodge Viper, and also son of the famous Southpole JFK successfully bred the first Apricot Snowshoe known worldwide.

In a council meeting on June 2013, Snowshoe Cats attained a full breed Status with the MEANING GCCF, mainly because of the undeniable team effort and dedicated breeders all over the UK. In October 2013 Snowshoes are officially allowed to be shown at Championship level with the GCCF.

The Snowshoe Cat, formerly known as Snowshoe Cat Association, was the first Snowshoe club to be established in the UK, then in April 2005 the Snowshoe Cat Society in United Kingdom was born.

Snowshoes are also fully recognized by the Fédération Internationale Féline, the American Association of Cat Enthusiasts, and the Cat Fanciers Federation.

Chapter Two: Before You Buy a Snowshoe

Are you now thinking of getting a Snowshoe cat? No problem! After knowing what they are, their behaviors, and how to deal with them, it's time to give you practical tips on what you need to know before buying one.

In this chapter, you will get a whole lot of information on its pros and cons, its average associated costs as well as the licensing you need so that you will be well on your way to becoming a legitimate Snowshoe pet owner -should you decide to be one! It's up to you! Read on!

Chapter Two: Before You Buy a Snowshoe

License Requirements

If you are planning to acquire a Snowshoe as your pet, there are certain restrictions and regulations that you need to be aware of. Licensing requirements for pets varies in different countries, regions, and states. In the United States there are no federal requirements for licensing either cats or dogs – these rules are regulated at the state level. While it is true that most states do not have a mandatory requirement for people to license their cats, it is always a good idea to do so because it will not only serve as protection for your pet but also for you.

Here are some things you need to know regarding the acquirement of Snowshoe cats both in United States and in Great Britain.

United States Licensing for Cats

The average annual license cost is $10.00. Cat licenses for senior citizens are $5.00. Costs may vary depending on state.

When you acquire license for your cat you will be given a cat number that can then be linked to your contact information. If your cat gets lost and someone finds it, its license can be used to track you down so that they'll be able to return to you your pet. Of course, this information will

Chapter Two: Before You Buy a Snowshoe

only be available if your cat wears a collar with an ID tag.

It is also ideal that four month old cats and up as well as indoor cats should still have a license because it is required by municipal law. Even those cats that never leave the house have a way of getting out through accidentally open doors, gates, or windows. Also, a natural disaster like an earthquake or fire may cause your pet to flee the safety of your property; having your Snowshoe pet has a license on its collar, will help reunite your lost pet with you.

If you want to apply for a cat license, you can search the website of your municipal or state government online. You will be able to download the application form and just follow the procedure. After filling up the form, you can mail it to their office together with a fee, in some states there is currently no fee for a cat license so make sure to check first and find out how much it cost.

Documentary requirements must be submitted before permanently getting a pet license. They are as follows:

- Residents must include the current rabies certificate,
- Proof of spay and neuter, and microchip (if applicable) to make the license current.

In most states, these are the main documents needed to get a cat license. There might be additional requirements that need to be submitted in other states. The license will be considered temporary status until all documents are received.

If you don't want to put a collar on your cat a good alternative option is to have it micro-chipped. A microchip serves the same function but they can be embedded under your cat's skin so that it won't be lost. The procedure for having your cat micro-chipped is very quick and painless.

Great Britain Licensing for Cats

In Great Britain, licensing requirements for pets are a little different than they are in the United States. There are no overarching licensing requirements for cats in the Great Britain but you will need to get a special permit if you plan to travel with your cat into or out of the country.

Your cat may also be subject to a quarantine period to make sure he isn't carrying a disease like rabies – rabies has been eradicated from Great Britain through safety measures like these so it is important to maintain them.

Chapter Two: Before You Buy a Snowshoe

Snowshoe Cats Behavior with Children and Pets

Generally, Snowshoe cats are lively and very interactive, that is why it's a perfect choice for families with children. There is actually no general rule when introducing your pet with other types of animals, sometimes they'll get along, sometimes they won't. Fortunately, Snowshoes tend to get along with other cat species as well as other pets like dogs. You can expect your cat to accept others but do so with caution so that they could easily warm up with their new animal friends.

Snowshoes have a reputation for learning and

performing tricks easily, and it usually appreciates the attention given from children and even strangers provided that they treat them politely and with respect.

How Many Snowshoe Cats Should You Keep?

Snowshoe cats do not like to be left alone, they easily get bored and they need lots of attention and interaction. If you work a full-time job or if you spend a lot of time away from home, then it is highly recommended that you get a companion for your Snowshoe cat. As stated earlier, they can get along with other cats and can also become friends with dogs and other household pets if properly introduces. Ideally one or two snowshoe cats is fine, just make sure that before you get another one, you can provide for the needs of both cats.

Chapter Two: Before You Buy a Snowshoe

How Much Does it Cost to Keep a Snowshoe Cat?

Owning Snowshoe cats doesn't come cheap! Generally, these cats are low maintenance but you still need to provide supplies and be able to cover the expenses in order to maintain a healthy lifestyle and environment for your pet. These things will definitely add up to your daily budget, the cost will vary depending on where you buy it, the brand, the nutrients included and the time being. If you want to own a Snowshoe as a pet you should be able to cover the necessary costs it entails.

Chapter Two: Before You Buy a Snowshoe

In this section you will receive an overview of the expenses associated with purchasing and keeping Snowshoes as pets such as food and treats, grooming and cleaning supplies, toys, veterinary care, and other costs so that you can determine whether you are able to provide for such a cat or not.

Initial Costs

The initial expenses associated with keeping Snowshoes as pets include the cost of the cat itself as well as the its bed, accessories, toys, initial vaccinations, micro-chipping or licensing, spay/neuter surgery as well as grooming supplies.

You will find an overview of these costs below as well as the estimated total expense for keeping one or two Snowshoes:

Purchase Price: starts at $300 - $1,200

The cost to purchase a Snowshoe cat can be quite expensive. You can adopt a rescue cat for as little as $150 - $400 sometimes but purchasing a kitten, especially a purebred kitten from a responsible breeder, could be much more costly. The cost of a show-quality Snowshoe cat or one that is a pure-bred with rare point colors is approximately as $300 - $1,200 or more on average.

Chapter Two: Before You Buy a Snowshoe

Cat Bed: more or less $50

Snowshoes are a medium-sized cat that's why you won't need a very large bed. Generally, the average cost for a normal size cat bed is about $50.

Food/Water Bowls or Dishes: more or less $30

In addition of providing your Snowshoe cats with a bed to sleep in, you should also make sure it has a set of high-quality food and water bowls. The best materials for these is stainless steel because it is easy to clean, cannot be easily chewed or eaten and won't acquire bacteria, another good option is ceramic. The average cost for a quality set of stainless steel bowls is about $30.

Toys: starts at $30

Like other pets, Snowshoes need plenty of stimulation to keep their intelligent and curious minds entertained. Keep cat boredom at bay with fun toys for your Snowshoes. To start out, plan to buy an assortment of toys for your cat until you learn what kind it prefers. Minimum cost of toys is approximately $30 or more, cost may vary depending on the brand.

Micro chipping: $50

In the United States and United Kingdom there are no federal or state requirements saying that you have to have your cat micro-chipped, but it is very ideal, as mentioned

Chapter Two: Before You Buy a Snowshoe

earlier, your Snowshoe could slip outside through an open door or window without you noticing it. If someone finds it without identification, they can take it to a shelter to have its microchip scanned. A microchip is something that is implanted under your cat's skin and it carries a number that is linked to your contact information. The procedure takes just a few minutes to perform and it only costs about $50 on average, but in some states cost may vary and there are certain documents that you may need to submit in your local government.

Initial Vaccinations: starts at $50

This is only applicable if you acquire a kitten, during your kitten's first year of life, it will require a number of different vaccinations. If you purchase your kitten from a reputable breeder, it might already have had a few but you'll still need more over the next few months as well as booster shots each year. Snowshoes can be susceptible to bacterial and viral infections such as panleukopenia, calicivirus, rhinotracheitis, and rabies, which are preventable through vaccination. You should include it in your budget which may cost at around $50 or more.

Spay/Neuter Surgery: approximately $50 - $200

If you don't plan to breed your Snowshoes you should have it neutered (for males) or spayed (for females) before 6 months of age. In females, this procedure includes

Chapter Two: Before You Buy a Snowshoe

surgically removing the ovaries and usually the uterus while in males, the testicles are surgically removed. Spaying or neutering your pet decreases the likelihood of certain types of cancers and eliminates the possibility of your pet producing an unwanted offspring. The cost for this surgery will vary depending where you go and on the sex of your cat.

If you go to a traditional veterinary surgeon, the cost for spay/neuter surgery could be very high but you can save money by going to a veterinary clinic. The average cost for neuter surgery is $50 to $100 and spay surgery costs about $100 to $200.

Accessories: average $70

There will be times that you may need to let your snowshoe cat outside the house or even present it for a show, that's why you might need several of cat accessories like a leash (if you're planning to train them or walk them outside) and other things like cat costumes or dresses, grooming materials during shows or simply repairing cat supplies. On average, extra accessories may cause at least $70 depending on brand and quality of the product.

Chapter Two: Before You Buy a Snowshoe

Cost	One Cat
Purchase Price	$300 - $1,200 (£223.60 - £894.41)
Cat Bed	$50 (£37.27)
Food/Water Bowl	$30 (£22.36)
Toys	$30 (£22.36)
Micro chipping	$50 (£37.27)
Vaccinations	$50 (£37.27)
Spay/Neuter	$50 to $200 (£37.27 - £149.07)
Accessories	$70 (£52.17)
Total	$630 to $1,400 (£469.57– £1,043.48)

*Costs may vary depending on location
**U.K. prices based on an estimated exchange of $1 = £0.75

Monthly Costs

The monthly costs associated with keeping a Snowshoe can be quite expensive. Some of the things that need to be bought on a monthly basis like food supplements, annual license renewal, toy replacements, and veterinary exams.

On the next page is an overview of each of these costs as well as an estimate for each cost.

Chapter Two: Before You Buy a Snowshoe

Food and Treats: $30

Feeding your Snowshoe cat a healthy diet is very important for its health and wellness. A high-quality diet for cats is not cheap and Snowshoe cats need moist foods to keep their physique. You should be prepared to spend around $30 for a high-quality cat food which will last you about a month. You should also include a monthly budget of at least $10 for treats.

License Renewal: $3 per month

The cost to license your Snowshoe cat is generally about $25 and you can renew the license for the same price each year, some states may cost more. License renewal cost divided over 12 months is about $3 per month.

Veterinary Exams: approximately $7 a month

As mentioned earlier, Snowshoes may get ill due to viral and bacterial infection, that's why you may need to take them to a vet for a medical check-up every now and then. In order to keep your cat healthy, you should take it to the veterinarian about every six months after it passes kitten hood.

You might have to take it more often for the first 12 months to make sure he gets his vaccines on time. The average cost for a vet visit is about $40. If in case, your cat get sick, it's better and wiser to set aside a portion of your budget for any medical needs that will come up.

Chapter Two: Before You Buy a Snowshoe

Additional Costs: at least $15 per month

In addition to all of these monthly costs you should plan for occasional extra costs like replacements for worn-out toys and cleaning products. You won't have to cover these costs every month but you should include it in your budget to be safe.

Cost	One Cat
Food and Treats	$30 (£22.36)
License Renewal	$3 (£2.24)
Veterinary Exams	$7 (£5.22)
Other Costs	$15 (£11.18)
Total	$55 (£40.99)

*Costs may vary depending on location

**U.K. prices based on an estimated exchange of $1 = £0.75

Chapter Two: Before You Buy a Snowshoe

Pros and Cons of Snowshoe Cats

The information listed below is the advantages and disadvantages of owning a Snowshoe cat:

Pros
- **Personality:** They are gentle, amiable and affectionate
- **Appearance:** Has a unique markings and very pleasing to the eye
- **Behavior:** Not aggressive and gets along with other cats
- **Hygiene:** Usually does its own natural grooming
- **Impact on Humans:** Loves children, high interactive and very loyal. A truly great companion.

Cons
- **Damage to Your Home**: They can ruin your furniture if they got bored.
- **Behavior:** Does not do well in isolation, needs lots of attention
- **Noise:** Very talkative, and has an opinion about everything.

Chapter Two: Before You Buy a Snowshoe

Chapter Three: Tips in Buying Snowshoe Cats

Now that you are already aware and have prior knowledge about the legal aspects of owning a Snowshoe as well as its pros and cons, the next step is purchasing one through a local pet store or a legitimate breeder.

In this chapter you will receive some basic tips for finding a Snowshoe breeder and for choosing one that is reputable and trustworthy. You will also receive tips for picking out a kitten that is healthy and well-bred.

Chapter Three: Tips in Buying Snowshoe Cats

Finding a Reputable Snowshoe Breeder

The first thing you need to do is to look for a legit cat breeder or pet store in your area that specializes in Snowshoe cats.

You can also find several Snowshoe cats or kittens breeders online but you have to take into consideration the validity of the breeder. It is highly recommended that you check first if they are associated with cat societies or organizations to ensure that they are legitimate and a good breeder. You can find several recommended list of Snowshoe breeder websites later in this book.

Be careful about purchasing kittens from pet stores because you do not know where they came from – they could come from a quality breeder but it is more likely they came from a hobby breeder or an unlicensed breeding facility that puts profits over the welfare of the animals.

The Cat Fanciers' Association (CFA) in the United States is a great website to search to learn how to breed Snowshoes. These organizations also provide useful information as well as recommendations especially when finding breeders.

In Great Britain and in other parts of Europe, The International Cat Association (TICA) also provides a list of breeders for each of its registered cat breeds. You can also try the Snowshoe Cat Society UK which provides a list of breeders as well.

Chapter Three: Tips in Buying Snowshoe Cats

If you don't particularly care about bringing home a Snowshoe kitten, or if you want to do your part in reducing the unwanted pet population, you might want to think about adopting a cat. There are many benefits for adopting Snowshoe cats besides the fact that you could literally be saving a life by taking a rescue cat into your home.

Many rescue cats have already been litter trained and they are often past the kitten phase as well, which means that you may not have to deal with typical kitten behaviors like scratching. Rescue cats that are adults are also fully grown and developed so you can get a good feel for their personality – kittens can change in terms of their personality as they mature so you never really know what you might end up with.

If possible, try to spend quality time with your prospect cat or kitten to see if you get along with one another.

a.) Choosing a Reputable Snowshoe Cat Breeder

The difference between a reputable breeder and a kitten producer is that the former spends large amounts of time and money on the best interest of the breed, while the latter is often motivated by profit.

In order to find a good Snowshoe breeder, however, you may have to do some research first.

Chapter Three: Tips in Buying Snowshoe Cats

Start by asking your local vet clinic or fellow cat owners for recommendations.

Once you've compiled a list of several Snowshoe breeders you then need to go through them to choose the best option. You don't want to run the risk of purchasing a kitten from a hobby breeder or from someone who doesn't follow responsible breeding practices.

On the next sections, you'll be given recommended websites on reputable breeders, once you have narrow down your list of breeders, you can go and check to see the best option for you.

b.) Snowshoe Breeders in the United States

Below is the list of Snowshoe breeders, rescue websites as well as the online directory from snowshoe cats associations in the United States:

United States Breeders List:

Local Breeders Directory:

Cat Fanciers' Association
<http://www.cfa.org/>

Purrpoints
<http://www.purrpoints.net/>

American Cat Fanciers Association

Chapter Three: Tips in Buying Snowshoe Cats

<http://www.acfacat.com/breeders_directory.htm>

Petfinder
<https://www.petfinder.com/cat-breeds/Snowshoe>

Breedlist
<http://www.breedlist.com/breeders/sno.html>

Breeders Traditional Cats
<http://www.breeders.traditionalcats.com/Breeders/traditional_snowshoe_catteries.htm>

United States Rescue and Adoption Websites:

Adopt a Pet
<http://www.adoptapet.com/s/snowshoe-cats-for-adoption>

Pure Bred Cat Rescue
<http://www.purebredcatrescue.org/>

c.) Snowshoe Breeders in Great Britain

Below is the list of local Snowshoe breeders, rescue websites as well as the online directory from snowshoe cats associations in Great Britain:

Great Britain Breeder's List

Chapter Three: Tips in Buying Snowshoe Cats

Local Breeders Directory and Snowshoe Association Websites:

The International Cat Association
<http://tica.org/nl/find-a-breeder>

Snowshoe Cat Society
<http://thesnowshoecatsociety.co.uk/?page_id=66>

Snowshoe Cats UK
<http://www.snowshoecatsuk.co.uk/>

Kitten List
<http://www.kittenlist.co.uk/breeders/search.php?bt=364>

Sapphire Star Cats
<http://www.sapphirestarcats.com/>

Destrier Cats
<http://www.destriercats.co.uk/er/item/423>

Chapter Three: Tips in Buying Snowshoe Cats

d.) Tips on How to Find a Reputable Cat Breeder

The Snowshoe cat is unfortunately quite hard to breed because of its lineage. Also there may be some health conditions involved when you buy a snowshoe kitten, so it is extremely important that you get your kitten from a reputable breeder. A reputable breeder will DNA-test his breeding stock to prevent passing these diseases on, he/she will also take other steps to ensure that his kittens are healthy and well-bred.

Here are some signs you should look out for when finding a reputable snowshoe cat breeder:

- The kittens should be bound by contract with the breeder.
- The breeder carefully interviews prospective owners and has specific requirements to be met.
- The breeder should be able to educate the novice. He/she happily answers questions regarding the breed and his/her breeding program.
- The cats/kittens should come with a health warrantee.
- There should also be a contract from the breeder to return cat/kitten should the buyer be unable to keep the cat/kitten. If they are unable to take the cat or kitten themselves, they will assist in finding a new home for the returned cat or kitten.

Chapter Three: Tips in Buying Snowshoe Cats

- The breeder should insist on being informed of health, genetic, or behavioral problems the cat/kitten may develop.
- The breeder should not have more cats/kittens than what he/she is able to keep clean, healthy and well socialized.
- The breeder should be concerned with the behavior and attitude of his/her cats/kittens.
- The breeder should always be available for advice and help to other breeders, and throughout the life of the cats/kittens he/she has placed.
- The breeder should spend quality time with each of his cats/kittens
- Visit the website for each breeder on your list (if they have one) and look for key information about the breeder's history and experience.
- Schedule an appointment to visit the facilities for the remaining breeders on your list after you've weeded a few more of them out.
- Put down a deposit, if needed, to reserve a kitten if they aren't ready to come home yet.

Chapter Three: Tips in Buying Snowshoe Cats

Selecting a Healthy Snowshoe

Snowshoes on average can live for up to 20 years and more! These breed are long time companions, and its longevity highly depends on how your chosen breeders took care of them especially when they were young.

This section will give you simple tips on how you can spot a healthy Snowshoe cat or kitten that you can keep for life!

a.) Signs of a Healthy Cat

- **Behavior:** Snowshoes should be active and playful, and loves to interact with people or with other pets
- **Body Appearance**: Kittens should not have difficulty in moving, otherwise they could be ill. Examine the kitten's body for signs of any illness and potential injury
- **Eyes:** The eyes should be clear and bright with no discharge.
- **Ears:** The ears should be clean and clear with no discharge or inflammation.
- **Belly or Stomach:** Look out for a distended or swollen tummy area.
- **Ability:** Find a kitten that can run or walk normally, and does not have any mobility issues.

Chapter Three: Tips in Buying Snowshoe Cats

- **Dealing with Humans:** Pick up the kitten and hold him to see how he responds to human contact.

Once you've chosen your healthy Snowshoe kitten or cat, ask the breeder about the next steps. Do not take the kitten home if it isn't at least 8 weeks old and unless it has been fully weaned and eating solid food. Any reputable breeder will not try to sell you a kitten that isn't already weaned or at least 8 weeks old.

Chapter Four: Maintenance for Snowshoe Cats

Assuming that you have already bought a Snowshoe as your pet, the responsibility that comes with it is the most crucial part of the process. You as the owner, have to provide for its basic needs so that it will be healthy and happy. In this chapter you will learn the different requirements needed for your cat such as its health requirements, accessories as well as how to keep it happy and healthy.

Chapter Four: Maintenance for Snowshoe Cats

Tips on How to Cat-Proof Your Home

Snowshoes, like any other cats are curious by nature, so it's important to cat-proof your house before bringing home your new pet, not only for its safety but also yours.

Here are some tips on how to prepare your home for your new found pet:

- **Remove any poisonous plants**- cats like to chew anything, if your cat chew any plants, even the non-poisonous ones can cause vomiting and diarrhea.
- **Keep away Cleaning Supplies** - cleaning supplies are dangerous and are definitely fatal to your cats.
- **Unplug your House-** Do not leave your appliances plugged, as mentioned earlier, they will chew anything including electric wires, not only is this potentially fatal for your cat but also a dangerous threat for your home.
- **Put a Lid on the Toilet -** a kitten will likely fall inside the toilet, so do not leave them unattended.
- **Do not leave Doors and Screens Unlocked** - Don't let your pet slip out and don't leave them unattended.

Chapter Four: Maintenance for Snowshoe Cats

Environmental Requirements for Snowshoe Cats

The Snowshoe cat is not your typical house cat. Many house cats are lazy, preferring to spend their days napping in the sun but Snowshoes are very lively and demands lots of attention. Your Snowshoe will need plenty of daily exercises in the form of active playtime and it will want to spend a lot of time with you as well. Make sure you can give your pet lots of attention otherwise it may not be the right breed for you.

In terms of its habitat requirements, what your cat really needs is lots of room to roam around with. It will also need plenty of stimulating and engaging toys to play with to help him work off its excess energy. Cats love to climb, so consider buying or building a cat tree for your Snowshoe. You can also install shelving on your walls to give your cat a place to perch, that way it can have an overview of the whole place and may feel secure. Just be careful about decorating your house with things that can be knocked over – cats are notorious for making a game of knocking things off shelves.

Your Snowshoe will not need a crate like a dog does, but you should provide it with a nice comfy bed. Many cat owners find that their cats do not actually sleep in their cat beds; they prefer to sleep in boxes or in other strange locations. To encourage your cat to use the bed, try sprinkling it with catnip.

Chapter Four: Maintenance for Snowshoe Cats

You may even want to keep several beds around the house in places your Snowshoe is likely to hang out like in a quiet room, under a window or in the living room.

Another environmental factor you need to consider for Snowshoe cats is the temperature. These cats do not have a thick coat of fur to keep them warm so the ambient temperature in your house should be a little warmer than what you might consider normal. You should also avoid exposing your Snowshoe to too much sunlight because it might cause skin or coat issues.

Toys and Accessories for Snowshoe Cats

Cats are naturally athletic animals that are why playing with toys is a vital activity, it improves their strength and agility. Playing is also important for mental and physical stimulation, it serves as an outlet for their natural hunting drive, and it's also a chance for them to bond with you. It's both fun and healthy for your pet.

Snowshoes are quite good at making themselves entertained, and you don't need to buy expensive toys in order to keep them stimulated, although sometimes it is also advisable because some toys are designed to develop certain physical aspects.

Chapter Four: Maintenance for Snowshoes

Aside from toys you can buy in pet stores, here are some examples of improvised or Do-It-Yourself toys you can find in your household to make your cat or kitten active and lively! You can be as creative and as interactive as you want to be when making activities with these things:

- Crumpled Ball of Paper
- Cork
- Ping pong balls or Golf balls
- Paper Bags
- Empty Cardboard Boxes
- Round Plastic Shower Curtains
- Flashlight
- Dangling Objects
- Stuffed toys (can be filled with catnip)

<u>Important Reminder:</u>

Before using the items above, remove any objects that your cat could chew or swallow such as ribbons, plastic bag, feathers, rubber bands, strings, paper clips, pins, tinsel, needles or other small decorations. If possible, always supervise your cat when he/she is playing and keep harmful objects out of reach

Chapter Four: Maintenance for Snowshoes

Tips in Keeping Your Cats Happy Indoors and Outdoors

It's a myth that going outside is a requirement for your Snowshoe's happiness, while it is true that letting your cat play or roam around outside may exercise their hunting skills, staying outdoors could potentially be harmful to your cat because of dangerous factors such as predators, and exposure to diseases.

Below are some tips you can do to keep your cat happy and stimulated by maximizing the benefits of letting it stay outdoors without the risks:

- Provide fences, a screened porch or a safe enclosure. Be sure to cat-proof your yard so that your cat could experience the outdoors safely.
- Buy a harness and train your cat to walk on a leash when going around the neighborhood
- Install padded perches indoors near a window frame or in your patio so that your pet could enjoy and hang out
- Consider buying a ready-made cat tree to provide climbing opportunities for your cat inside.
- Plant cat grass inside your house where your cat can graze

Chapter Five: Nutritional Needs of Snowshoe Cats

Feeding your Snowshoe is not that complicated. However, its level of activity should be taken into consideration to meet its nutritional diet. They're not choosy eaters but it is highly recommended that cats, like many other pets, should be given a recommended food for a balanced nutrition because proper diet can lengthen the life

Chapter Five: Nutritional Needs of Snowshoe Cats

expectancy of your cat.

In this section, you'll learn the majority of your pet's nutritional needs as well as feeding tips and foods that are good and harmful.

Essential Nutrients

a.) Protein

Generally cats' bodies can't produce essential amino acids on their own. Amino acids are the building blocks of life and these provide energy. Cats can get most of their protein from meat, fish, and other animal products. Some animal-based protein is easier to digest than plant-based protein and is better suited to the cat's digestive system.

For kittens, recommended amount is 10 grams, while adult cats need about 12.5 grams of protein daily. See pet food labels when buying cat food.

b.) Fats and Fatty Acids

Essential fatty acids are necessary to keep your cat's skin and coat healthy. Lack of fatty acids can lead to different problems and abnormalities of the nervous system. Dietary fats, can usually be found in animal fats and the seed oils of various plants, Fatty acids play an important role in cell structure and function. Fats provide the most concentrated source of energy in the diet.

Chapter Five: Nutritional Needs of Snowshoe Cats

For kittens, recommended amount is 4 grams, while adult cats need about 5.5 grams of fatty acids or fats daily.

c.) Calories

This nutrient is one of the main sources of energy among cats and even humans. You can find calories in several commercial cat foods such as cereals, legumes and other vegetables.

For kittens (after weaning), recommended daily caloric intake is 200 pounds, while daily caloric intake for adult cats ranges from 170 - 1,091 pounds depending on their weight.

d.) Vitamins

Lack of vitamins can cause different illnesses, this organic compound is important not only to help prevent health issues but also to aid in a variety of metabolic activities.

Unfortunately some canned food lacks certain vitamins like Vitamin E, which provides protection against oxidative damage. If it is given in excess amount, it can be toxic to your cat. Consult your veterinarian to see the specific vitamin your cat needs and follow the right amount for it.

Chapter Five: Nutritional Needs of Snowshoe Cats

e.) Minerals

There are twelve essential minerals that you need to include in your cat's diet. These minerals mainly provide are crucial in creating strong bones and teeth, for muscle contraction and nerve impulse transmission and to prevent formation of stones as well as to provide necessary enzyme's that your cat's body needs. These are the following minerals your cat needs to intake daily:

- Calcium
- Phosphorus
- Magnesium
- Potassium
- Sodium
- Selenium
- Copper
- Chlorine
- Iron
- Copper
- Zinc
- Iodine
- Manganese

*Consult with your veterinarian if you need to know the specific vitamin your cat needs as well as the amount needed for each

Chapter Five: Nutritional Needs of Snowshoe Cats

f.) Water

Hydration is just as important for cats as it is for human beings especially during hot weather conditions to avoid dehydration. However, cats don't drink as much as water as dogs does, mainly because of their evolution as desert animals. Still, our cat should be given access to clean, fresh and cool water. Inability to provide clean water to your cat can cause upset stomach with unbearable stomachache.

Water is vital to maintain cells, digestion, coat, skin and metabolism.

Toxic Foods to Avoid

Some foods are specifically toxic for your Snowshoes or even cats in general. Make sure that your cat never gets to eat one of the toxic items below and ensure that the veterinary checks your cat every now and then. These harmful foods is as important as selecting the right supplements and food items for your cat.

The following list of foods is highly toxic for your Snowshoe cats:

- Alcohol
- Apple seeds
- Avocado
- Cherry pits
- Chocolate

Chapter Five: Nutritional Needs of Snowshoe Cats

- Coffee
- Garlic
- Grapes/raisins
- Hops
- Macadamia nuts
- Mold
- Mushrooms
- Mustard seeds
- Onions/leeks
- Peach pits
- Potato leaves/stems
- Rhubarb leaves
- Tea
- Tomato leaves/stems
- Walnuts
- Xylitol
- Yeast dough

Chapter Five: Nutritional Needs of Snowshoe Cats

Types of Commercial Cat Foods

There are three major types of commercial cat foods; these are dry, semi moist, and canned. Dry food contains 6 to 10% moisture, semi moist is 15 to 30% and canned is 75%. Most canned food has relatively more fat, protein and animal products and lesser carbohydrates than dry and semi-moist food.

Pet food labels must list the percentage of protein, fat, fibre, and water in the food. Ask your veterinarian on how to properly read pet food labels so that you can get the most out of the food.

Chapter Five: Nutritional Needs of Snowshoe Cats

Food Additives

There are other substances that are not required but may also help in your cat's health such as the following:

- **Chondroprotective agents** - which is mostly used by the body to make cartilage and joint tissues.
- **Antioxidants** - which are known to prevent oxidative damage nutrients
- **Herbs** - known to have medicinal effect on the body
- **Flavors and Extracts** - derived from animal tissues such as poulty and fish

Tips in Selecting a High-Quality Cat Food Brand

The task of choosing a high-quality cat food can be difficult for some cat owners simply because there are so many different options to choose from. If you walk into your local pet store you will see multiple aisles filled with bags of cat food from different brands and you may also notice that most brands offer a number of different formulas. So how do you choose a healthy at food for your Snowshoe cat without spending hours and money at the pet store?

The best place to start when shopping for cat food is to read the cat food label. Pet food in the United States is loosely regulated by the American Association of Feed

Chapter Five: Nutritional Needs of Snowshoe Cats

Control Officials (AAFCO) and they evaluate commercial pet food products according to their ability to meet the basic nutritional needs of cats in various life stages. If the cat food product you are looking at contains this statement you can move on to reading the ingredients list.

Cat food labels are organized in descending order by volume. This means that the ingredients at the top of the list are used in higher quantities than the ingredients at the end of the list. This being the case, you want to see high-quality sources of animal protein at the beginning of the list because protein is the most important nutrient for cats. Things like fresh meat, poultry or fish are excellent ingredients but they contain about 80% water.

After the product is cooked, the actual volume and protein content of the ingredient will be less. Meat meals (like chicken meal or salmon meal) have already been cooked down so they contain up to 300% more protein by weight than fresh meats.

In addition to high-quality animal proteins, you want to check the ingredients list for healthy fats and a limited amount of digestible carbohydrates. In terms of fat, you want to see at least one animal source such as chicken fat or salmon oil.

Plant-based fats like flaxseed and canola oil are not necessarily bad, but they are less biologically valuable for your cat. If they are accompanied by an animal source of fat, it is okay. Just make sure that the fats included in the recipe

Chapter Five: Nutritional Needs of Snowshoe Cats

provide a blend of both omega-3 and omega-6 fatty acids. This will help to preserve the skin condition of your Snowshoe cat.

For cats, digestible carbohydrates include things like brown rice and oatmeal, as long as they have been cooked properly. You can also look for gluten-free and grain-free options like sweet potato and tapioca. It is best to avoid products that are made with corn, wheat, or soy ingredients because they are low in nutritional value and may trigger food allergies in your cat.

You also want to avoid commercial cat foods that contain a large amount of carbohydrates since the cat's body is not adapted to digesting plant materials as effectively as animal products. Cats only need a very small amount of fiber.

In addition to checking the ingredients list for beneficial ingredients you should also know that there are certainly things you do NOT want to see listed. Avoid products made with low-quality fillers like corn gluten meal or rice bran – you should also avoid artificial colors, flavors, and preservatives.

Some commonly used artificial preservatives are BHA and BHT. In most cases the label will tell you if natural preservatives are used.

When reading the label for commercial cat food products you need to be careful about taking health claims and marketing gimmicks with a grain of salt. Just because

Chapter Five: Nutritional Needs of Snowshoe Cats

the label includes words like "natural" or "holistic", you cannot make assumptions about what those terms actually mean since the definitions are not regulated for pet foods like they are for people food.

It's important to check for the AAFCO statement of nutritional adequacy as well as the ingredients list instead of just trusting what the manufacturer says about the product.

How to Feed Your Snowshoe Cats

Whether you have a finicky or overzealous eater, your cat's needs to be fed properly and it's also important that you have fun doing so! Below are some tips on how to properly feed your cat so that feeding time can be more effective and enjoyable.

The purpose of a cat's whiskers is that it is use to navigate its surroundings, as well as determine the width of openings, and even communicate mood.

Here are tips for choosing a dish that is suitable for your cat's whiskers:

- Choose a dish large enough to hold a day's worth of food, with a lip just tall enough to keep the food contained while letting your cat easily observe the room.

Chapter Five: Nutritional Needs of Snowshoe Cats

- If you constantly find yourself cleaning up after your cat, consider a wide plate large enough to catch stray kibble or canned food.

- Use a shallow bowl that your cat can grab food from without impeding the whiskers.

Dish Placement

Where you place the dish plays an important role in your cat's level of comfort at feeding time. Below are some tips on the ideal and recommended location of your cat's dish or bowl:

- Try placing the dish in the open to maximize sight lines. It also helps lessen the tension.

- Do not place your cat's dish in the corner of a room or on an edge because it's difficult to see the surroundings. This is also recommended with multiple cats or a dog.

Feeding Accessories

A puzzle feeder or a food distributor ball is ideal especially if your cat is overweight or has a tendency to eat a lot of food in just one sitting. These accessories are also great for enhancing the curious and intelligent minds of cats.

Chapter Five: Nutritional Needs of Snowshoe Cats

- You can find such accessories at your local pet store or even online. Its cost vary depending on the brand of the product

- Both puzzle feeders and food distributor balls fuel up your cat's desire to hunt and work search for food.

- Always check the feeders after use to make sure your cat is actually eating the recommended daily amount of food.

Benefits of Side-Chewing

A fun fact about cats in general is that they chew food with their back teeth, particularly when working on larger pieces of food. Some people interpret this as difficulty chewing and fear the cat may choke.

Here are some tips if your cats do side-chew:

- The side-chewing technique lets your cats enjoy different textures and may also help clean the molars in the process.

- Don't discourage side-chewing. In reality, your cat is simply using the best teeth for the job.

Chapter Five: Nutritional Needs of Snowshoe Cats

- Follow the Feeding Instructions and Recommended Daily Feeding Amounts on the packaging of your pet food. You can also consult your veterinarian regarding the feeding measurement.

- Place the recommended measured amount of food inside the bowl or dish each morning so your cat can eat as he or she pleases throughout the day.

- Monitor your cat's weight and adjust intake accordingly. The amount of food required to maintain an ideal body condition will vary depending on age, activity and environment.

- For energetic cats, try dividing the daily portion into several bowls and place them in different locations throughout your home. This also helps to encourage your cat to discover sources of food throughout the day.

- Reduce the daily intake of dry food to prevent overfeeding. Only if you feed your cat a combination of dry and wet food.

- Monitor the water intake to make sure your cat is properly hydrated.

Chapter Five: Nutritional Needs of Snowshoe Cats

- For kittens, it is highly recommended that you begin offering moistened dry food at 3 - 4 weeks old and make it available to them at all times through the weaning stage at 6 - 8 weeks old.

- To help keep the food fresh and encourage your kitten to eat only moisten one of these servings at a time rather than preparing the entire daily amount at once and leaving it out all day for grazing.

- Also use warm water for your kittens.

Chapter Five: Nutritional Needs of Snowshoe Cats

Chapter Six: Caring Guidelines for Snowshoe Cats

In this chapter, you will learn lots of tips on how to generally care for your Snowshoe cat. You'll learn how to train them, groom and clean them, and even get some tips if you'd like to maybe present them to others through joining cat shows. These things are essential in making your pet's lifestyle as fun and wonderful as it can be. It'll make you a better owner if you know your cat's strength and weaknesses.

Chapter Six: Caring Guidelines for Snowshoe Cats

Socializing Your Cat

The Snowshoe cat is naturally interactive and outgoing breed, but you still need to socialize them to ensure that they become well-adjusted to different environments. If you don't give your Snowshoe cat or kittens plenty of new experiences it might respond to new situations with fear or anxiety.

Fortunately, socialization for Snowshoe cats is easy to grasp. Below are some tips on how to socialize your cat so that it'll feel confident and at ease with others.

- Introduce your cat/kitten to friends in the comfort of your own home where your cat/kitten feels safe.

- Take your cat with you to the pet store or to a friend's house so that it experiences new locations.

- Expose your cat/kitten to people of different sizes, shapes, gender, and skin color.

- Introduce your cat/kitten to children of different ages. Just supervise the kids to make sure they handle the cat/kitten safely.

Chapter Six: Caring Guidelines for Snowshoe Cats

- Take your cat/kitten with you in the car when you run errands, make them part of your daily routine as much as possible.

- Expose your cat/kitten to loud noises such as fireworks, cars backfiring, loud music, and thunder. It will get used to it eventually.

- Introduce your cat/kitten to various appliances and tools such as blenders, lawn mowers, vacuums, etc.

- Play with your cat/kitten using different kinds of toys and experiment with different kinds of food and treats to also see its preferences.

Training Your Snowshoe Cats

At some point in time, you and your pet will already get along and are comfortable in each other, strengthen your relationship by training them.

Training a Snowshoe is not that hard to do, in fact it can be a fun and rewarding bonding experience for both of you.

There are lots of pet owners out there who have properly trained and raised a well-behaved Snowshoe. They are intelligent creatures by nature, that is why they can

Chapter Six: Caring Guidelines for Snowshoe Cats

absorb information very quickly and easily as long as you do it right.

Trust is the most important key in training your cat. The first thing you need to do is to be able to establish a solid connection and rapport between you and your pet.

This section will provide some guidelines you can follow in getting your Snowshoe cat well behaved and disciplined. Are you ready? Read on!

Here are some tips on how to train your cat:

- Decide on the suitable hand signal. Whistling and hand clapping are ideal because you can give the signal at any time.

- Avoid using bells or other signaling devices, because it may not be effective during emergencies.

- Train your cat when it is hungry. You can offer some treats if it follows a command from you. For best results, keep repeating this exercise until the cat/kitten gets used to it.

- Teach your cats different commands such as positions and litter box training. Use food treats or positive reinforcement once it follows and repeat the exercises over and over again.

Chapter Six: Caring Guidelines for Snowshoe Cats

Litter Training for Snowshoe Kittens

For the most part, kittens learn to use the litter box from their mothers so you may not have to do any litter training for your Snowshoe cats at all. You will, however, have to make sure that you teach the kitten the location of the litter box and give him some time to get used to it.

When you bring your kitten home, take your kitten to the litter box and place him inside. He may scratch around a little bit or he might jump right out – either is fine. Just keep putting your kitten in the litter box a few times a day for the first few days until he gets used to the location. You should also make sure that it is in a quiet, easy to reach location.

Chapter Six: Caring Guidelines for Snowshoe Cats

If you have more than one Snowshoe cat, you should also have more than one litter box. The best rule of thumb to follow is one litter box per cat plus one extra. Some cats do not mind sharing litter boxes but others will refuse to use one that another cat has used. Some cats also use one litter box to urinate and another to defecate. Set up your litter boxes in a quiet, private place that is easy to access. If you have a dog in the house you may need to place the box somewhere he can't get to it – some dogs will eat clumps out of the litter box.

There are many different types of litter boxes to choose from so you have plenty of options. Just be sure that the box you choose is large enough for your cat to get into and move around in easily.

In terms of the type of litter, most cats prefer fine-textured litter to coarse litter. You should keep about 2 inches of litter in the box at all times and scoop it frequently and refresh it with new litter. It is usually best to keep less litter in the box and to clean it more often than to use a lot of litter. Just be careful not to choose a litter that is too dusty or one that has too much fragrance added to it – these things could aggravate allergies in your Snowshoe cat.

Chapter Six: Caring Guidelines for Snowshoe Cats

Here are some quick tips on how to train your cat to use a litter box:

- Place a clean litter box where your cat likes to hang out or in a confined area such as a room in your house, living room corner etc.

- Be sure your cat has plenty of food and clean water.

- It is also effective to put the waste of your cat in its own litter box or at least near it so that it won't go outside of the box and will be aware of the smell.

- Usually within a day or two of being confined with the litter box the cat will begin to use the box regularly.

Behavioral Problems

Snowshoe cats are very smart and very active. While this is usually a good thing, it can sometimes lead to trouble. If your cat doesn't get the exercise or attention he needs, he could become destructive in the house or he might develop other problem behaviors like urinating outside the litter box or scratching the furniture. This cat breed does have some dog-like qualities but you cannot train them to the same

Chapter Six: Caring Guidelines for Snowshoe Cats

degree that you can train a dog. Still, there are some things you can do to help curb problem behaviors.

The Snowshoe cat is very affectionate and he will always be paying attention to you when you spend time together – he will take his cues from you and watch how you react to the things he does. If your Snowshoe cat does something you don't like, you should not punish him for it. It is very unlikely that your cat will connect the punishment to the crime and he might just end up being afraid of you. Instead, you need to either teach your cat that bad behaviors don't earn him the attention he wants or you should provide a more suitable outlet for the behavior.

When it comes to things like scratching, you should not try to completely eradicate this behavior. Scratching is a normal and important behavior for cats because it helps them to stretch their toes and to spread their scent through glands in the pads of their feet. If your Snowshoe cat is scratching up your furniture, the solution may be as simple as providing him with scratching posts around the house. To encourage your cat to use them instead of your furniture, sprinkle them with dried catnip or use a liquid catnip spray. When your cat uses the scratching post, give him a couple of treats as well to encourage him.

Sometimes Snowshoe cats can develop a tendency toward demanding attention – they are also known to become very vocal when they want something. It is important to understand that this is a characteristic of the

Chapter Six: Caring Guidelines for Snowshoe Cats

breed so you may not be able to change it. You can, however, reduce annoying behaviors like incessant meowing by not giving in to your cat. If he meows at you for attention and you give it to him you will only be reinforcing that behavior. If you want your cat to leave you alone while you are working on the computer, for example, just ignore him until he gives up. Eventually your cat will learn when it is play time and when it is not

Grooming Snowshoe Cats

Your Snowshoe cat's skin produces natural oils that help to protect his skin and to keep it moisturized. Grooming for cats is not just about keeping it clean, it is mainly about improving and maintaining the condition of the skin. Grooming your cat helps to distribute its natural body oils to keep his skin healthy, shiny, and soft.

Generally cat should take a bath about once or twice a week. If you do it regularly, your cat will get used to it and it will not become a major chore.

To bathe your Snowshoe, fill your tub or a large sink with about 1 inch (2.54 cm) of lukewarm water – you only need enough to get his skin damp. Use a baby shampoo or something that is very mild and fragrance-free and massage it into your cat's skin by hand or using a soft cloth.

Chapter Six: Caring Guidelines for Snowshoe Cats

When you are finished bathing, use a soft cloth and some warm water to remove all traces of soap. Once your cat gets used to the bathing process it may tolerate you pouring water over his back to rinse it.

How to Brush Your Cat's Teeth

Periodontal disease can cause health issues in cats that is why it is important in keeping your cat's teeth clean. Many cat owners neglect their cat's dental health which is a serious mistake. Brushing your cat's teeth is fairly easy, though you will need a special pet tooth brush and pet toothpaste to do it – you may also need to get your cat accustomed to the toothbrush and the tooth-brushing process slowly. Ideally you should be brushing your cat's teeth every day but if he will only let you do it a few times a week then that is certainly better than nothing.

How to Trim Your Cat's Nails

Your cat's nails grow in the same way that your own nails grow so they need to be trimmed occasionally. Most pet owners find that trimming their cat's nails once a week or twice a month is sufficient. Before you trim your Snowshoe's nails for the first time you should have your veterinarian or a professional groomer show you how to do it.

Chapter Six: Caring Guidelines for Snowshoe Cats

A cat's nail contains a blood vessel known as "quick." The quick supplies blood to the nail, and if you cut the nail too short you could sever it. A severed quick will cause your cat pain and it will bleed profusely. The best way to avoid cutting your cat's nails too short is to just trim the sharp tip.

Cleaning Your Cat's Ears

Snowshoe cats have a quite normal, open ear, that's why you do not have to worry as much about ear infections as you might with other breeds. Ear infections are most common in breeds that have folded ears because it limits the amount of air flow to the inner portion of the ear and wet ears are a breeding ground for bacteria. It is still ideal to clean your Snowshoe cat's ears occasionally just to remove normal wax buildup.

To clean its ears, use a cat ear cleaning solution and squeeze a few drops into the ear canal. Then, massage the base of your cat's ears to distribute the solution, and then wipe it away using a clean cotton balls.

Presenting Your Snowshoe Cat

The Snowshoe cat is a recognized breed for both the Cat Fanciers' Association (CFA) and The International Cat Association (TICA) which means that it is eligible for pedigreed show. Showing your cat can be a wonderful but

Chapter Six: Caring Guidelines for Snowshoe Cats

challenging experience and it is also a great opportunity to spend more time with your cat, which could strengthen your bond. Learning how to show your cat properly can take time, so do not expect to win your first show.

This section will give you a highlight about the Snowshoe breed standard and some general show guidelines.

Snowshoe Cat Breed Standard

The Snowshoe cat is a beautiful and unique breed that is accepted and recognized by the Cat Fanciers' Association (CFA), The International Cat Association (TICA), American Association of Clinical Endocrinologists (AACE), and American Cat Fanciers Association (ACFA).

The breed standards for each of these organizations vary but this section will give you the ideal and general guidelines on the Snowshoe cat breed standard.

Chapter Six: Caring Guidelines for Snowshoe Cats

Head Breed Standard

- Wide as it is long
- Triangular, however, may be slightly rounded (apple head shape like traditional cat head)
- Medium size
- Good proportion and visual balance with the rest of the body
- High set cheek bones
- Nose of good length, neither extremely broad nor extremely pointed and in proportion to the rest of the head
- Forehead should be a flat plane rising slightly above the muzzle giving the appearance of two distinct, parallel planes, no less than the width of an eye between the eyes
- When the whiskers are smoothed back, the underlying bone structure is evident with allowances for stud jowls in older males
- Ears are medium to medium-large with slightly rounded tips
- Exhibits striking black or black-based color points

Coat Breed Standard

- Short-haired
- Solid and white patterns

Chapter Six: Caring Guidelines for Snowshoe Cats

- Points are on ears, tails, face-mask, and sometimes the legs are black or black-based colors
- Body has an even coloration with subtle shading to point color on the back
- Patterns vary, however, will typically fall along the face, chest, stomach, and paws

Paws Breed Standard

- Paw pads may be white, point color, flesh tone or mottled with the color and darkening with age, even to the point of turning a chocolate brown shade. Snowshoe cats come in blue, lilac, lynx, fawn, chocolate and seal points.

Preparing Your Snowshoe Cat for Show

Showing your Snowshoe cat can be a wonderful experience but it can also be quite challenging. In order to ensure that your cat does well in the show, he needs to be a strong example of the breed standard. Make sure that you familiarized yourself with the rules and regulations for the particular show in which you plan to enter your cat.

In addition to making sure that your cat meets the qualifications of the breed standard, there are also some general things you can do to prepare for a cat show.

Chapter Six: Caring Guidelines for Snowshoe Cats

Here are some tips to help prepare you and your cat for show:

- Make sure your cat is properly pedigreed according to the regulations of the show – you may need to present your cat's papers as proof so be sure to have them ready.

- Make sure to fill out the registration form correctly, providing all of the necessary details, and turn it in on time – you may also have to pay an entry fee at this time.

- Clip your Snowshoe cat's claws before the show – declawed cats are allowed as well without penalty.

- Make sure that your cat is registered with the organization running the show.

- Be sure to enter your cat in the proper age bracket or category - some organizations allow kittens as young as 3 months.

- Find out what is provided by the show and what you need to bring yourself – some competitions provide an exhibition cage but you will need to bring some things.

Chapter Six: Caring Guidelines for Snowshoe Cats

Important reminder:

Below are the lists of things you need before the show:
- Your cat's pedigree and registration papers.
- Veterinary records and proof of vaccinations.
- Litter pan and cat litter (if not provided).
- Food, treats, and food/water bowls.
- Cage curtains and clips to hang them.
- A blanket or bed for the cage.
- Any necessary grooming equipment, nail clippers.
- Confirmation slip received at entry.
- Food, water, and extra clothes for yourself.
- Garbage bag for clean-up.

Be prepared to spend all day at the show and bring with you everything you and your cat need to make it through the day. Some shows provide a list of recommended materials to bring so pay close attention to all of the information the show gives you with your registration.

Chapter Seven: Breeding Snowshoe Cats

If you decided to buy two cats, for instance a male and female and keep them together, you should definitely prepare for the possibility of breeding, unless it's the same gender, otherwise you're going to be caught off guard!

If you are interested in breeding your Snowshoes, this chapter will give you a wealth of information about the processes and phases of its breeding and you will also learn how to properly breed them on your own. This is not for everyone but if you want to have better understanding about how to raise these cats, then you should definitely not miss this part!

Chapter Seven: Breeding Snowshoes

On the contrary if you are interested in becoming a reputable breeder, then this is a must read chapter for you.

Basic Cat Breeding Information

In general, cats have an estrous, or heat cycle. The queen (female cats) can enter her first heat or sexual maturity as young as 4 months, and she generally has 2 or 3 heat cycles during the breeding season, which usually occurs around February to October in the northern hemisphere. Female cats are induced ovulator, which basically means that they do not ovulate unless they are bred. This greatly increases the chances of conception when bred.

There are many signs that the queen is undergoing its heat cycle such as rolling, rubbing against objects, and kneading her back feet, and yowl repeatedly and loudly. If you notice your Snowshoe doing this, that means that she is ready for mating.

This behavior can last 3 to 20 days and can repeat in 10 to 40 days if the queen is not bred. If the queen is bred, the cycle ends as her body prepares for pregnancy.

In the feline world, pregnancy is called gestation. Gestation lasts for about 60 to 63 days or within 2 months. Its average litter size is about 4 – 6 kittens. Queens can be bred by more than one male during a heat period, the semen of male cats can stay inside the queen for a period of time even

Chapter Seven: Breeding Snowshoes

if the queen or female cat have already mated with other male cats, resulting in kittens from the same litter with different fathers.

Signs that your cat is pregnant:

- Large abdomen
- Increased appetite
- Swollen mammary glands (that may release milk when squeezed)

During the later stages of pregnancy, the queen seeks a nesting area and places bedding in a quiet, secluded spot. Make sure to provide your cat with a comfortable bed, feed it properly and don't disturb it as much as you can, so that it can produce healthy offspring.

Pseudo pregnancy is also called false pregnancy for cats. This typically begins at the end of estrus and can last for several months. Consult your veterinarian to determine if your cat is pregnant for real or not.

Mating Behavior of Cats

Queen or female cats will repeatedly call a tom cat (male cat) when she is ready to mate with him. Another sign is that the queen sprays during their heat cycle to spread the smell of their readiness for mating. Once a tom cat sniffs it,

Chapter Seven: Breeding Snowshoes

he will stay and linger around the queen until mating happens.

Male cats also respond to the queen in certain voice that is a call for mating. Whenever a queen will hear this call, she would run towards it. This whole communication or invitation of cats for mating is highly dependent on calling by these specific sounds.

Mating Time Period

The mating may last for about 5 - 10 minutes or even more. You will know that the mating is over, if the queen shrieks out loud. Once done, the female cat would do it again if she is ready, as long as she is still in her heat cycle; otherwise, she won't entertain or pay attention in any tom cat after the cycle was finished.

Usually a queen would keep on licking herself and gets ready for another mating session. The interval between mating sessions could be around 30 minutes or even few hours. It is also not necessary that a female cat would go back to the same tom cat next day. As mentioned earlier, this could result in producing kittens with multiple fathers.

Chapter Seven: Breeding Snowshoes

Labor Process of Cats

During labor, time between contractions decreases typically around 2 to 3 minutes apart. The first kitten to be born takes about 30 minutes to 1 hour after strong contractions and the birth interval between kittens is usually 15 minutes to 30 minutes.

Upon giving birth the kitten is inside a placenta and wrapped in the amniotic sac membranes that will cover its muzzle. The mother cat should break these by licking to enable the kitten to breath.

Chapter Seven: Breeding Snowshoes

The mother cat will also chew through the cord and eat the placenta, which is normal and nutritionally valuable for her, although quite gross for us humans.

If you want to help in giving birth to your pet, make sure you have the following:

- Watch or clock
- Clean cloth or toweling face
- Small box
- Polar fleece, baby blanket etc. and hot water bottle
- Gloves
- Fresh bedding
- Scissors

But before helping during the labor process, consult your veterinarian first or study and ask breeders on how to do this properly.

Here are some signs that your snowshoe is ready to give birth:

- Presence of water bubble of amniotic fluid – indicates that a kitten is in the birth canal

- The queen cries out or move around to make itself comfortable

Chapter Eight: Keeping Your Cat Healthy

You as the owner should be aware of the potential threats and diseases that could harm the wellness of your Snowshoes. Just like human beings, you need to have knowledge on these diseases so that you can prevent it from happening in the first place. You will find tons of information on the most common problems that may affect your cat including its causes, signs and symptoms, remedies and prevention.

Chapter Eight: Keeping Your Cat Healthy

Common Health Problems

In this section, you will learn about the diseases that may affect and threaten your snowshoe's wellness. Learning these diseases as well as its remedies is vital for you and your cat so that you could prevent it from happening or even help with its treatment in case they caught one.

Below are some of the most common health problems that occur specifically to Snowshoe cats. You will learn some guidelines on how these diseases can be prevented and treated as well as its signs and symptoms.

Heart Disease

HCM or otherwise known as Hypertrophic Cardiomyopathy is a muscle disease in the heart wherein the heart muscles thicken and blocks arteries. Another common form of heart disease among cats is called DCM or Dilated Cardiomyopath; it is a secondary disease that also damages the heart

Causes

HCM is caused by an overactive thyroid gland, while DCM is caused by a lack of amino acid Taurine.

Signs and Symptoms

Common signs of this disease are rapid breathing, lethargy, and a poor appetite. Usually, symptoms don't

Chapter Eight: Keeping Your Cat Healthy

appear, until it's too late. The cat has actually been suffering for several days to weeks before physical signs of this disease appear.

Recommendation:

Most cats with cardiomyopathy have a heart murmur that can be detected during a wellness physical exam. It is highly recommended that you let your cat undergo through a genetic testing to detect a specific gene abnormality that may cause HCM and DCM. Usually a specific diagnosis requires more advanced medical imaging. The best treatment is to detect it early that is why it is important to have your cat be screened at least twice a year.

Arterial Thromboembolism

This disease is also known as FATE or Feline Aortic Thromboembolisms. If your cats has this disease it will eventually develop blood clots in their arteries usually found just part of the aorta, the large blood vessel that supplies blood from the heart to the body. It blocks the normal blood flow to the hind legs, which causes paralysis of both hind legs and sometimes even become cold or painful.

Signs and Symptoms

The main sign that your cat is suffering from FATE is its sudden inability to walk or if the cat is dragging one or both hind legs and crying. Once you notice this, seek

Chapter Eight: Keeping Your Cat Healthy

medical care as soon as possible, your pet needs emergency care because it is fatal.

Treatment

FATE is a life-threatening disease, so as soon as you learned that your cat is suffering from this disease, consult a veterinarian immediately because this requires quick action and prolonged medical care. Cats who survive thromboembolisms, however, usually regain full function of their limbs. If your cat is diagnosed with heart disease, veterinarians may prescribe medications to help lower the risk of blood clots.

Feline Lower Urinary Tract Disease (FLUTD)

This disease is the inability to control the bladder muscles, which is usually due to improper nerve function from a spinal defect. Urinary defect is rare in cats so if you notice that your cat is urinating in improper locations, it may be suffering from FLUTD and is trying to get you to notice.

Symptoms

Watch out for any signs of abnormal urination such as urinating on a tile floor, bathtub or any other cool surface. Some early symptoms also include a blood in the urine; small amount or no urine at all as well as unusual crying in the litter box. Cats that are previously diagnosed with

Chapter Eight: Keeping Your Cat Healthy

urinary tract infection, bladder stones or urolithiasis are also prone to Feline Lower Urinary Tract Disease.

Recommendation:

If your cat demonstrates any of these symptoms, bring it to a veterinarian right away, because this can become an emergency within only a few hours. The inability to urinate is painful and quickly fatal, especially for male cats, if its urethra is blocked with stones or crystals, the urine will be blocked.

An important reminder to prevent such disease is to always bring your cat to a clinic for a regular urinalysis testing. This test allows us to check for signs of infection, kidney disease, crystals in the urine, and even diabetes. You can also perform other tests such as X-rays and ultrasounds because it can also help detect the presence of stones in the bladder or kidneys.

If you brought your pet early to the vet, lower urinary tract disease can be controlled with medications and special diets, though in some severe cases of FLUTD it may also require surgery.

Renal Failure

Renal failure is another fatal disease that can evolve from previous urinary tract problems, this is the inability of the kidneys to properly drain toxins and cleanse the waste in the blood. If your cat has renal failure it will not properly perform its function of regulating hydration. Kidney disease is extremely common in older cats.

Cause

This disease is often due to exposure to toxins or genetic causes in young cats. It is hereditary and passed on from one generation to another. Even very young kittens can have renal failure if they have inherited kidney defects from their mothers and fathers.

Recommendation:

The best preventive measure is to perform screening tests for kidney problems as early as 2 months old, make sure to also regularly screen your pet throughout its entire lifetime because sometimes, it doesn't show up in the first few test. Severe renal failure is a progressive, fatal disease, sometimes called a "slow death" but special diets and medications can help cats with kidney diseases live longer, fuller lives if treated early.

Hyperthyroidism

Cats with these tumors have their metabolic switch permanently stuck in a constant fast-producing position. This illness is termed hyperthyroidism, wherein the thyroid gland produces a hormone called thyroxine, or T4. Thyroxine regulates the overall speed of metabolic processes throughout the body.

Chapter Eight: Keeping Your Cat Healthy

This disease is common among middle-aged cats about ten to twelve years of age, they developed a benign (non-cancerous) tumor in the thyroid gland. The cells that make up this tumor still produce T4, but their control mechanism is faulty. The normal feedback system that maintains a balanced T4 level in the body has no effect on these tumor cells, so that they continue to pump out T4 despite signals to stop, resulting in a more active cat, with a nervous energy that covers their illness they are feeling.

Signs and Symptoms

The typical symptoms are vomiting, weight loss, and increased thirst but these signs are sort of asymptomatic and only show on progressively but in a gradual pace, that's why the problem is not easily noticed. In advanced cases, hyperthyroidism can lead to heart failure, kidney failure, and fatal blood clots if not treated early.

Recommendation and Treatment

A standard blood test can easily detect if your cat potentially can develop hyperthyroidism, these sample tests should be performed as part of your cat's routine wellness plan.

Veterinarian's treat this disease by killing off the abnormal tumor cells while leaving the normal thyroid cells undamaged, resulting in a normal and sometimes longer life

Diabetes Mellitus

Diabetes Mellitus is a genetic and hereditary disease that can occur in any cat breed. Cats can be diabetic regardless of other health problems. Other cats may have a susceptibility to diabetes, but will only become overtly diabetic if they are allowed to become overweight or eat a poor diet. If a cat's weight and diet are managed appropriately, the risk for diabetes in your pet is much lower.

Cause

The main cause of diabetes in cats is inactive lifestyles. If your cat just likes to eat a lot and be lazy all the time, it may be the root cause of this disease that is why exercise is very important to prevent diabetes.

Signs and Symptoms

Major symptom of diabetes includes weight loss despite of a good appetite, excessive thirst, and increased urination. It is also ideal to undergo some tests for at least once a year and more often as your cat ages, because older cats are much prone to becoming diabetic.

Chapter Eight: Keeping Your Cat Healthy

Treatment

The worst case scenario is that your cat may need insulin injections to treat its diabetes, but usually many diabetic cats do not need to receive insulin injections if they lose weight, they just need to switch to a high-protein, low-carbohydrate prescription diet. Diabetes are thought to be hereditary especially among Snowshoes, that is why managing the type and quantity of food that your pet eats and incorporating exercise into your cat's daily routine is very vital!

Recommendation

Daily exercise and proper diet is key in keeping your cat active and energetic. If your cat is slim or fit, it can highly prevent illnesses related to weight gain. Diabetes can also be related to a painful condition called pancreatitis. Chronic pancreatitis, which is thought to be genetically inherited, can lead to damage of the cells in the pancreas that produce insulin, and therefore can lead to a diabetic state in the cat. Always consult your veterinarian if you feel like your cat is suffering from diabetes.

Allergies/Atopy

Cats, like humans can suffer from an itchy skin. This form of allergy in cats is known as "atopy." The affected areas are the legs, belly, face, and ears

Chapter Eight: Keeping Your Cat Healthy

Signs and Symptoms

Symptoms of atopy are licking or over grooming the affected areas, rubbing its face and regular ear infections. Sometimes, you may notice thinner or shortened hair as well as sore skin lesions. Such signs usually appear between 1 to 3 years old and can get worse every year.

Treatment

Mites may also be the cause of the problem since they have similar signs. The great thing is that there are many treatment options available for this condition. Consult your veterinarian to know the best treatment for your cat's atopy.

Recommended Vaccinations for Snowshoes

Like all cats, Snowshoes are susceptible to different bacterial and viral infections which are fortunately preventable through vaccination. Core Vaccines are highly recommended if the risk of your cat contracting these diseases is high.

In addition, vaccines are available to offer protection from other potential dangerous diseases like feline leukemia and other fatal virus.

The vaccination recommendations listed below for your cat, highly depends on the availability in your area,

Chapter Eight: Keeping Your Cat Healthy

your cat's age, and any other risk factors specific to its lifestyle:

- **Panleukopenia**
  Class: Core
  Efficacy: High
  Length of Immunity: More than 1 year
  Risk/Severity of Adverse Effects: Low to Moderate

- **Rhinotracheitis**
  Class: Core
  Efficacy: High; reduces severity but not prevent disease
  Length of Immunity: More than 1 year
  Risk/Severity of Adverse Effects: Low
  Remarks: Use intranasal vaccine for faster protection

- **Calicivirus**
  Class: Core
  Efficacy: Variable; reduces severity but not prevent disease
  Length of Immunity: More than 1 year
  Risk/Severity of Adverse Effects: Low
  Remarks: May see sneezing in cats

- **Rabies**
  Class: Core
  Efficacy: High

Length of Immunity: Depends on the type of vaccine
Risk/Severity of Adverse Effects: Low to Moderate
Remarks: Lower for recombinant vaccines

- **Feline Leukemia**
  Class: Recommended
  Efficacy: Variable
  Length of Immunity: Needs revaccination
  Risk/Severity of Adverse Effects: Vaccine-related sarcoma can develop with killed vaccines
  Remarks: Vaccine is not recommended for cats with minimal or no risk

- **Chlamydophila**
  Class: NonCore
  Efficacy: Low
  Length of Immunity: Less than 1 year
  Risk/Severity of Adverse Effects: High
  Remarks: Vaccine is not recommended for cats with minimal or no risk

- **Feline Infectious Peritonitis**
  Class: NonCore
  Efficacy: Low
  Length of Immunity: Unknown
  Risk/Severity of Adverse Effects: Unknown
  Remarks: Not recommended but can be ideal

Chapter Eight: Keeping Your Cat Healthy

- **Bordetella**
  Class: NonCore
  Efficacy: Low
  Length of Immunity: Short
  Risk/Severity of Adverse Effects: More severe in kittens

- **Giardia**
  Remarks: Not recommended, upon advised by veterinarian

- **Feline Immunodeficiency Virus**
  Remarks: Not recommended unless your cat has been identified with FIV. Upon advised of the veterinarian.

Vaccination Schedule for Cats and Kittens

For kitten aged 6 - 7 weeks old, combination of vaccines, which is consists of feline distemper, rhinotracheitis, and calicivirus is needed. For kittens that are 10 weeks old, combination of vaccines is needed plus Chlamydophila or Pneumonitis, because during this age, they are prone to respiratory diseases.

For kittens that are 12 - 13 weeks old and up (age may vary according to local law), generally they need to have a rabies vaccine as well as feline leukemia vaccine (FeLV), because at this age kittens can be exposed to feline

Chapter Eight: Keeping Your Cat Healthy

leukemia virus, these vaccines can be given by your local veterinarian.

For adult cats, aside from combination of vaccines booster, cats also need Chlamydophila or Pneumonitis vaccine, feline leukemia vaccine (FeLV), as well as rabies vaccine.

Consult with your local veterinarian to determine the appropriate vaccination schedule for your cat. Remember, recommendations vary depending on the age, breed, and health status of the cat, the potential of the cat to be exposed to the disease, the type of vaccine, whether the cat is used for breeding, and the geographical area where the cat lives or may visit.

Signs of Possible Illnesses

- **Sneezing** - does your cat have nose discharge?
- **Dehydration** - does your cat drink less than the usual? It may be a sign that there is something wrong with your cat
- **Obesity** - is your cat showing signs of obesity? It may be prone to a heart disease, or diabetes. Monitor your cat's weight before it's too late.
- **Elimination** - does your cat regularly urinate and defecate? Always check its litter to make sure that its stool and urine is normal. Contact the vet

Chapter Eight: Keeping Your Cat Healthy

immediately if there are any signs of bleed and diarrhea.
- **Vomiting** - does your cat vomits and is it showing signs of appetite loss?
- **Coat** - does its coat and skin still feels soft, fluffy and rejuvenated? If your cat is sick sometimes, it appears physically on its body.
- **Paws/Limbs** - does your cat have trouble walking or is it only dragging its legs? It could be a sign of paralysis.
- **Eyes** - are there any discharge in the eyes?
- **Overall Physique** - does your cat stays active or are there any signs of weakness and deterioration?

Chapter Eight: Keeping Your Cat Healthy

Chapter Nine: Snowshoe Cats Checklist

Congratulate yourself! You are now on your way to becoming a very well-informed and pro-active Snowshoe cat owner! Finishing this book is a huge milestone for you and your future or present pet cat, but before this ultimate guide comes to a conclusion, keep in mind the most important things you have acquired through reading this book.

This chapter will outline the summary of what you have learned, including the checklist you need to keep in mind to ensure that you and your Snowshoe lived happily ever after!

Chapter Nine: Snowshoe Cats Checklist

Basic Cat Information

- **Pedigree**: very talkative, short coat, average shedding, pointed colors
- **Breed Size**: medium to medium-large (normal size)
- **Height:** 9 - 11 inches
- **Weight**: average 10 to 14 pounds
- **Physique:** medium-sized, muscled
- **Coat Length**: short
- **Skin Texture**: soft and smooth
- **Color:** blue, lilac, lynx, fawn, chocolate, and seal points
- **Eyes**: blue colored eyes
- **Ears**: very large (2 to 3 inches tall), wide at the base
- **Tail**: medium in length; rounded tip
- **Temperament**: very energetic and interactive, sweet, affectionate and loyal
- **Strangers**: needs warming up and proper introduction
- **Children**: can bond with children
- **Other Pets**: gets along with other cats and most other pets
- **Exercise Needs**: Playing with toys
- **Health Conditions**: generally healthy but prone to some conditions such as panleukopenia, calicivirus, rhinotracheitis, and rabies,

Chapter Nine: Snowshoe Cats Checklist

feline leukemia virus (FeLV).
- **Comparable Breeds:** California Spangled Cat, Norwegian Forest Cat, Egyptian Mau
- **Lifespan:** average 15 to 20 years

Nutritional Needs

- **Nutritional Needs:** amino acids or protein, fatty acids, calories, vitamins, minerals, water
- **Amino Acids:**
- **Amount to Feed (kitten):** 10 grams
- **Amount to Feed (adult):** 12.5 grams
- **Fatty Acids:**
- **Amount to Feed (kitten):** 4 grams
- **Amount to Feed (adult):** 5.5 grams
- **Calories:**
- **Amount to Feed (kitten- after weaning): 200 punds**
- **Amount to Feed (adult):** ranges from 170 - 1091 pounds depending on weight, age and activity
- **Important Vitamins:** Vitamin A, D, E, K, Thiamin, Riboflavin, Vitamin B6, Niacin, Pantothenic Acid, B12, Folic Acid
- **Amount to Feed:** Consult with your veterinarian if you need to know the specific vitamin your kitten or cat needs as well as the amount needed for each
- **Important Minerals:** Alcohol, Apple seeds, Avocado,

Chapter Nine: Snowshoe Cats Checklist

Cherry pits, Chocolate, Coffee, Garlic, Grapes/raisins, Hops, Macadamia nuts, Mold, Mushrooms, Mustard seeds, Onions/leeks, Peach pits, Potato leaves/stems, Rhubarb leaves, Tea, Tomato leaves/stems, Walnuts, Xylitol, Yeast, dough

- **Amount to Feed:** Consult with your veterinarian if you need to know the specific vitamin your kitten or cat needs as well as the amount needed for each
- **Cat Food Types:**
- **Dry:** 6 - 10% moisture
- **Semimoist:** 15 - 30% moisture
- **Canned:** 75% moisture
- **Food Additives:** Chondroprotective agents, Antioxidants, Herbs, Flavors and Extracts
- **Feeding Frequency:** included in daily meal serving or depending on your vet's recommendation.

Breeding Information

- **Mating Period:** 5 – 10 minutes
- **Sexual Maturity (female):** average 5 to 6 months
- **Sexual Maturity (male):** 8 to 9 months
- **Breeding Age (female):** 12 months, ideally 18 to 24 months
- **Breeding Age (male):** at least 18 months

Chapter Nine: Snowshoe Cats Checklist

- **Breeding Type**: seasonally polyestrous, multiple cycles per year
- **Ovulation**: induced ovulation, stimulated by breeding
- **Litter Size**: about 4 – 6 kittens
- **Birth Interval**: 15 – 30 minutes
- **Pregnancy**: average 50 - 60 days
- **Kitten Birth Weight**: 80 to 100 grams (0.2 to 0.22 lbs.)
- **Eyes/Ears Open**: 8 to 12 days
- **Teeth Grow In**: around 3 to 4 weeks
- **Begin Weaning**: around 4 to 6 weeks, kittens are fully weaned by 8 weeks
- **Socialization**: between 8 - 10 weeks, ready to be separated by 13 weeks

Cat Accessories

- **Food and Water Bowls:** Stainless or Ceramic
- **Toys:** dangling objects that provide stimulation
- **Cat Bed:** Normal size
- **Other accessories:** leash, grooming and cleaning materials etc.

Chapter Nine: Snowshoe Cats Checklist

Index

A

AAFCO	65
amino acid	11
antibodies	13
attention	53, 79, 80, 88

B

bathing	82
bed	53, 88
blood	83
body	12, 13, 14, 49, 66
breed	12, 13, 14, 15, 16, 53, 74, 79, 81, 83, 84, 86
breed standard	84
breeder	11, 12, 46, 47, 48
breeding	12, 13, 14, 15, 47, 83, 116

C

carbohydrates	65, 66
Cat Fanciers Association	12
cattery	11
CFA	12, 83, 84
children	74
claw	13
coat	11, 12, 13, 14, 16, 54, 66
color	12, 13, 14, 15, 16, 74
condition	66, 81
cut	83
cycle	13

D

desexed	11, 16

destructive 79
diet 11
disease 82
DNA 14, 47
dog food 64
dogs 66, 78
domestic 14

E

ear infections 83
ears 13, 15, 83
energy 53
essential 11
estrus 11
exercise 53, 79

F

face 12, 13, 14, 15
family 14, 15
fat 65
fatty acids 66
feet 14, 15, 80
female 11, 13, 14, 15, 16, 115
fertile 13
fiber 66
food 14, 64, 65, 66, 75, 88
food allergies 66
friendly 74
fur 14, 15, 54

G

genetic 11
groomer 82
grooming 88

H

health 66, 82
history 48

I

illness 49
infection 11
information 48
ingredients 65, 66
intact 15, 16

J

judge 11

K

kittens 14, 47, 77, 87, 116

L

lactating 13
life stages 65
litter 77, 78, 79, 88
litter box 77, 78, 79

M

male 11, 12, 15, 16, 115
markings 11, 12, 14, 15
meals 65
meat 65
milk 13
mite 11

mutation 11

N

nails 82
needs 65
neutered 11
nose 14, 15
nutrients 13

O

offspring 12, 13
oil 65

P

pattern 11, 13, 16
pedigree 12, 14, 88
pet 64
pigmentation 11, 13
play 81
preservatives 66
problem behaviors 79
protein 11, 65
punishment 80
purebred 15

R

requirements 53

S

scratching 79, 80
show 11, 15, 82, 83, 84, 86, 87, 88

signs 49
skin 11, 15, 16, 74, 81
socialization 74
standard 12, 13, 15, 84, 86
sunlight 54

T

tail 13, 15
teeth 82
temperature 54
The International Cat Association 83, 84
TICA 83, 84
training 77
traits 16
treats 75, 80, 88
trimming 82

V

vocal 80

W

walk 64
weaned 116
weight 65

PHOTOS

Page 9 Photo by user Arnaud Dessein, via Flickr.com, <https://www.flickr.com/photos/adessein/7598747510>

Page 17 Photo by user Steve Voght, via Flickr.com, <https://www.flickr.com/photos/voght/2258847755>

Page 25 Photo by user Steve Voght, via Flickr.com, <https://www.flickr.com/photos/voght/2258970825>

Page 29 Photo by Admin, via Catscutes.blogspot.com <http://catscutes.blogspot.com/2015/12/cat-breed-snowshoe.html>

Page 31 Photo by user Jeffrey Beall, via Flickr.com, <https://www.flickr.com/photos/denverjeffrey/16272601753>

Page 41 Photo by user Bernie H., via Flickr.com, <https://www.flickr.com/photos/hapa_princess/9438173515>

Page 51 Photo by user Bernie H., via Flickr.com, <https://www.flickr.com/photos/digallagher/231524886/>

Page 57 Photo by user sha in LA, via Flickr.com, <https://www.flickr.com/photos/72465344@N00/3641561399>

Page 63 Photo by Admin, via PGAA.com, < http://pgaa.com/index.php/feeding-organic/>

Page 72 Photo by user Michael Frank Franz, via Flickr.com, <https://www.flickr.com/photos/nwater/14266928079>

Page 76 Photo by user Michael Frank Franz, via Flickr.com, <https://www.flickr.com/photos/nwater/8183210605>

Page 88 Photo by user Michael Frank Franz, via Flickr.com, <https://www.flickr.com/photos/nwater/9621979676>

Photo 92 by user Steve Voght, via Flickr.com, <https://www.flickr.com/photos/voght/2258741103>

Page 95 Photo by Peggy Montgomery, via Purrpoints.net <http://www.purrpoints.net/>

Page 110 Photo by user Martin Pitchford, via Flickr.com, <https://www.flickr.com/photos/66342487@N02/16968894737>

REFERENCES

"**Basic Cat Training**" LoveThatPet.com
<https://www.lovethatpet.com/cats/behaviour-and-training/cat-training-tips/>

"**Breeding and Reproduction of Cats**" MerckVetManual.com
<http://www.merckvetmanual.com/pethealth/cat_basics/routine_care_and_breeding_of_cats/breeding_and_reproduction_of_cats.html>

"**Breeding From Your Siamese Cat – Finding the Right Stud Cat**" Pets4Homes.co.uk
<http://www.pets4homes.co.uk/pet-advice/breeding-from-your-siamese-cat-finding-the-right-stud-cat.html>

"**Caring for Your Feline Companion**" BrandonLakesAnimalHospital.com
<http://www.brandonlakesanimalhospital.com/client-resources/breed-info/snowshoe/>

"**Cat Proofing Your House**" HumaneSociety.org
<http://www.humanesociety.org/animals/cats/tips/cat_proofing_your_house.html?credit=web_id103701348>

"**Cat Tips**" HumaneSociety.org
<http://www.humanesociety.org/animals/cats/tips/>

"**Feline Diet & Nutrition**" Pets.Webmd.com

<http://pets.webmd.com/cats/guide/diet-nutrition-feline>

"**How to Train a Cat: Tips and Tricks**" Purina.com.au
<http://www.purina.com.au/cats/training/train>

"**Snowshoe Breed**" Catster.com
<http://www.catster.com/photoviewer/breed/Snowshoe"http://www.catster.com/photoviewer/breed/Snowshoe>

"**Snowshoe Cats Breed**" Cattime.com
<http://cattime.com/cat-breeds/snowshoe-cats#z5UWtI6BSz1KVJTP.99>

"**The Decision to Breed**" PetEducation.com
<http://www.peteducation.com/article.cfm>

"**Tips for a Healthy Cat**" Aspca.org
<https://www.petfinder.com/cats/cat-health/tips-healthy-cat/>

"**Vaccines & Vaccination Schedule for Cats & Kittens**" PetEducation.com
<http://www.peteducation.com/article.cfm>

"**Your Cats Nutritional Needs: A Science-Based Guide for Pet Owners**" Nap.edu
<http://nap.edu>

Feeding Baby
Cynthia Cherry
978-1941070000

Axolotl
Lolly Brown
978-0989658430

Dysautonomia, POTS Syndrome
Frederick Earlstein
978-0989658485

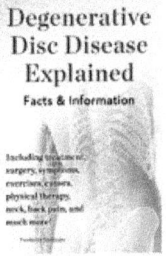

Degenerative Disc Disease Explained
Frederick Earlstein
978-0989658485

Sinusitis, Hay Fever,
Allergic Rhinitis Explained
Frederick Earlstein
978-1941070024

Wicca
Riley Star
978-1941070130

Zombie Apocalypse
Rex Cutty
978-1941070154

Capybara
Lolly Brown
978-1941070062

Eels As Pets
Lolly Brown
978-1941070167

Scabies and Lice Explained
Frederick Earlstein
978-1941070017

Saltwater Fish As Pets
Lolly Brown
978-0989658461

Torticollis Explained
Frederick Earlstein
978-1941070055

Kennel Cough
Lolly Brown
978-0989658409

Physiotherapist, Physical Therapist
Christopher Wright
978-0989658492

Rats, Mice, and Dormice As Pets
Lolly Brown
978-1941070079

Wallaby and Wallaroo Care
Lolly Brown
978-1941070031

Bodybuilding Supplements
Explained
Jon Shelton
978-1941070239

Demonology
Riley Star
978-19401070314

Pigeon Racing
Lolly Brown
978-1941070307

Dwarf Hamster
Lolly Brown
978-1941070390

Cryptozoology
Rex Cutty
978-1941070406

Eye Strain
Frederick Earlstein
978-1941070369

Inez The Miniature Elephant
Asher Ray
978-1941070353

Vampire Apocalypse
Rex Cutty
978-1941070321

www.ingramcontent.com/pod-product-compliance
Lightning Source LLC
Chambersburg PA
CBHW071706040426
42446CB00011B/1937